BLOCKCHAIN

Quickly Learn Blockchain and Its Role in Cryptocurrency—How Blockchain Technology Will Revolutionize the Digital Economy and Beyond

Copyright © 2017, 2018- By Lee Sebastian
All rights reserved.

Published By:
Positive Impact Books
7579 E. Main Street
Suite 500
Scottsdale, AZ 85251

Sign Up To Be Notified of Our Next Cryptocurrency Book Releases and Free Promotions.

www.PositiveImpactBooks.com

DISCLAIMERS

The following Book is reproduced below with the goal of providing information that is as accurate and reliable as possible. Regardless, purchasing this Book can be seen as consent to the fact that both the publisher and the author of this book are in no way experts on the topics discussed within and that any recommendations or suggestions that are made herein are for entertainment purposes only. Professionals should be consulted as needed prior to undertaking any of the action endorsed herein.

This declaration is deemed fair and valid by both the American Bar Association and the Committee of Publishers Association and is legally binding throughout the United States.

Furthermore, the transmission, duplication or reproduction of any of the following work including specific information will be considered an illegal act irrespective of if it is done electronically or in print. This extends to creating a secondary or tertiary copy of the work or a recorded copy and is only allowed with express written consent of the Publisher. All additional right reserved.

The information in the following pages is broadly considered to be a truthful and accurate account of facts and as such any inattention, use or misuse of the information in question by the reader will render any resulting actions solely under their purview. There are no scenarios in which the publisher or the original author of this work can be in any fashion deemed liable for any hardship or damages that may befall them after undertaking information described herein.

Additionally, the information in the following pages is intended only for informational purposes and should thus be thought of as universal. As befitting its nature, it is presented without assurance regarding its prolonged validity or interim quality. Trademarks that are mentioned are done without written consent and can in no way be considered an endorsement from the trademark holder.

Table of Contents

Introduction To Blockchain 1

Chapter 1: Blockchain Explained...3

Chapter 2: A Decentralized Economy 9

Chapter 3: How and Why Blockchain Works..12

Chapter 4: Bitcoin and Cryptocurrency Applications..15

Chapter 5: How Blockchain is Changing Money..19

Chapter 6: Blockchain and E-commerce 22

Chapter 7: How Blockchain Could Change the Future Economy 26

Chapter 8: What are Autonomous Agents 30

Chapter 9: Distributed Autonomous Agents and Its Dangers.....................34

Chapter 10: A Possible Future "Skynet"..39

Chapter 11: Government's Response to Blockchain and Cryptocurrency. 45

Chapter 12: Criminal Applications with Blockchain..51

Chapter 13: Banks and Financial Institutions with Blockchain...................55

Chapter 14: How to Profit with Blockchain 59

Chapter 15: How to Prepare for a Blockchain Economy 64

Chapter 16: Using Blockchain for Remaining Anonymous.........................68

Chapter 17: Decentralized Blockchain Technology 74

Conclusion 78

Helpful Links and Resources..78

INTRODUCTION TO BLOCKCHAIN

The world of finance has changed in recent times.

What used to work great for small local economies is now outdated and doesn't provide us with the efficiency that we need. It can take forever to get a transaction processed, even if it is all done online, and the costs of bookkeeping, improper transactions and more can really overwhelm small businesses.

Blockchain is ready to change all of that. Introduced with the advent of Bitcoin and other cryptocurrencies, the blockchain is a digital ledger that can help spin off transactions in just a few seconds while keeping them secure and safe for those who are using the system. It is unlike anything that the modern financial world is using, but it is exactly what the financial world needs right now.

Blockchain may be relatively new, but it is definitely changing the face of many parts of our economy. While many people may have only heard about it from using cryptocurrency, there is a big shift in how it will react to our current e-commerce and the current economy. This book is going to explore more about blockchain and how it can provide security while making online purchases, how it is decentralized to protect against banks and government agencies messing with it, and even how blockchain is going to change the way that we do business in the future.

When you are ready to learn more about blockchain and how it works, or how it will change our future, make sure to read through this book and learn everything that you need to know to get started with blockchain.

CHAPTER 1

BLOCKCHAIN EXPLAINED

Before we can get into some of the information on how blockchain is used, it is important to understand what blockchain is all about. To keep it simple, blockchain is a public ledger that shows all the transactions that have ever been done in cryptocurrency. It will keep growing as the completed blocks are added to it and each of these blocks will contain new information about transactions. Each block has to be added to the chain in a linear order that is chronological.

When a computer connects to the Bitcoin or other cryptocurrency networks, they will become one of the nodes and will receive a copy of the blockchain. This is going to download automatically (so the user won't have to take any additional steps), once the user has joined the network. This blockchain will hold onto all the information about balances and addresses of the transactions from the time the user starts making these transactions all the way to the most recent transaction.

The blockchain is a huge innovation in technology for Bitcoin because it holds all the proof that a transaction occurred. A block is going to be considered the current part of the blockchain that will be in charge of recording some of the recent transactions for the user. Once the block is done, it will be added in with the blockchain and become a permanent part of the database. Each time a block is completed, a new one will be created so that the transactions can be taken care of. When the blocks are added into the blockchain, they are going to be linked together in chronological order and how the previous block is stored will determine how this block is stored.

This may seem a little bit confusing, but we can use some conventional banking analogies to help. When we are talking about the blockchain, we are talking about a full history of all the banking transactions at a conventional bank. The transactions with Bitcoin are going to be entered into the blockchain chronologically, just like your bank transactions are. Each block in the blockchain can be compared to your bank statements.

Based on the protocol that is given with blockchain, the database is going to be shared by all the nodes, or computers, that are participating in transactions with this cryptocurrency. If you look at the full copy of the blockchain, you will find that it holds all the records for any and all transactions that have ever been done with Bitcoin. This makes it very valuable because it can show a lot of facts about who is making transactions, who has the most value, and so on.

Some people are worried about the growth of blockchain in the future. In the past, there haven't been as many transactions with Bitcoin, but since this and other cryptocurrencies are growing, it is likely that the blockchain could get large and congested. There could be some issues with the synchronization and storage of the blockchain and whether it will be able to keep up with the growing command.

The blockchain has made it so much easier for transactions to be accounted for and stored with cryptocurrency. But let's take a look in more detail about what blockchain is and how it can work to help not only in the world of cryptocurrency, but in finances, energy, and so much more.

What is a blockchain?

First, let's take a look at what blockchain is all about. This is actually a pretty wide term that covers many new technologies. There is some confusion about this definition since the technology is so new and there are so many different ways that the blockchain can be implemented based on what you would like to accomplish.

At a higher level, this type of technology is going to make it easier for a group of computers to agree, at intervals that are set up ahead of time, on the true state of a distributed ledger. These ledgers may contain a variety of shared data, including credentials, information on the transactions, transaction records, and more. With the help of game theory and cryptography, the ledger will remain secure and you won't have to worry about using some trusted nodes like with some other networks. This is why Bitcoin is able to transfer values throughout the globe without needing to rely on a bank or another intermediary to help them out.

On the blockchain, all the transactions that go through will happen chronologically, and they will link together to form an immutable chain. For the most part, you will be able to keep your information private and even anonymous depending on the way that you implement this technology. To keep it safe, the ledger will be placed in many areas on the network rather than in just one place. Copies will exist and will be updated with every node that is participating in the ecosystem.

Each of the blocks on the blockchain is going to hold onto important information and many types of data can be stored inside them. You could have information on property titles, identity, intellectual property, digital rights and even currency inside these blocks.

Right now, the blockchain is most commonly used with Bitcoin and other cryptocurrencies. Because of the way that it is set up, this technology is perfect for keeping track of the transactions that go on with these cryptocurrencies, allowing people from across the world to interact, receive money, and make purchases without having to work with a bank or another source. The blockchain is one of the big reasons that Bitcoin and these other online currencies have done so well in the past few years.

This doesn't mean that blockchain couldn't be used in other places to help change the way our economy works and we are going to spend some time talking about this in this book. Some of the industries that could be changed with the use of blockchain technology include:

- **Central banks: many banks throughout the world are considering using blockchain technology** to help make them more efficient. This could reduce their risk, make it easier to collect payments and fees, save money, and can help with payments across borders.

- **Finance**: this is one of the busiest areas for blockchain so far. Many finance companies like this technology because it helps with verifying international payments. It is secure, low cost, and can help them be more efficient with their work.

- **Money transfers**: some of the traditional money transfers in today's banking world can take days but with the help of blockchain, it can be done in just a few seconds, speeding up this process.

- **Micropayments**: instead of having to subscribe to an online news site to read a few articles, how would it be if you could only pay for the ones that you want. Your web browser could keep track of the pages that you read. Or what if you would get some smaller payments for work and you could get it right away. Blockchain could help to make this possible.

- **Identity and privacy**: the Silk Road, a black-market type place for online shopping, showed how easy it was to keep purchases and buyers private with Bitcoin and blockchain. There are some issues with this such as criminal activity, but for the average shopper, this can help to keep them safe.

- **Smart contracts**: this is something that is just getting started, but the smart contracts are ones that could use the information to make themselves self-executing once conditions are met. Both parties can agree to the conditions without needing the middleman.

The world of finance, banking, and our economy is ready to change, and at the front of all this could be blockchain technology. Let's read some more of the things that this technology could help us with in the future and how it is going to change so many things.

CHAPTER 2

A DECENTRALIZED ECONOMY

When we think of our economy, we usually think of one where all the businesses and buyers come together to make a profit. The sellers will offer jobs to help with this and then provide a product that consumers are able to purchase. The consumers get to have some say in the way that things are priced based on the purchases that they make. While it may seem like a free market system, the government and the banks are often behind it in, helping to slow it down or speed it up in some way.

For example, it is not uncommon for a government to change the rate of inflation to hinder or encourage the growth of businesses. Banks and governments are the ones in charge of setting the interest rates for borrowers and other entities, so they do have a lot of control over things. When things are done in the proper way, this can be a good way to keep a country from growing too rapidly or it can ensure that the country is not going to enter into a depression.

Of course, there are a lot of people who don't want the government or the banks meddling in the transactions that they are doing. They don't like the idea of letting the government control what is going on inside of the economy and they worry that the banks could make it more likely that an economy is going to fail. Because of these issues, the idea of a decentralized economy has come around thanks to Bitcoin and other cryptocurrencies.

The idea of cryptocurrency has changed this idea though. Instead of having a bank or a government behind them, the currency is going to have some code behind it. In many cases, such as with Bitcoin, there is a limited amount of Bitcoin available and no one can print or make more than what the code was designed for.

Only a little bit of the cryptocurrency was originally released in the beginning. In order to get more Bitcoin, miners are able to work on the blockchain and when they are successful, they will be able to earn more Bitcoin and add more to the community. But there are still only a limited amount of Bitcoin available and once those are all mined, that will be all that is inside the economy.

Many people like the idea of a decentralized economy. They are tired of having to worry about how a government is going to handle money and how inflation and other factors will make the value of their money worth less than it was when they received the money. With the help of the blockchain, Bitcoin and other cryptocurrencies are able to expand and have their own economy, with proof of transactions so everyone stays safe and secure, but without a centralized force behind them.

This is also why cryptocurrency has been able to grow all over the world. It doesn't matter where you are located before you can join Bitcoin or other cryptocurrencies. Since it is not centralized, you can switch any of your current currencies over to the cryptocurrency and make the payments, purchases, and more that you would like.

In a world where the government will often mess with the economy and the money of their countries to benefit themselves, it is nice to have a currency that doesn't have this kind of backing behind it. Some people are going to be worried about this, but most of the cryptocurrencies like Bitcoin will use safety features, like the blockchain, to help keep things organized and to ensure that transactions go smoothly.

CHAPTER 3

HOW AND WHY BLOCKCHAIN WORKS

The blockchain is a really cool piece of technology that you are able to use to help with transactions when using cryptocurrency. It was first used with Bitcoin, but it has grown over time to include the same idea when working with other types of cryptocurrency.

The blockchain is perfect for being able to work with these cryptocurrencies, although the technology that is behind it could easily be used in a lot of other applications over time. The blockchain is able to keep track of a lot of different information, usually financial information, so that it is easy to see when purchases were completed and both parties, the buyer, and the seller, can keep track of things. Right now, blockchain is used primarily in the cryptocurrency world, but it has the potential to be used in banking and other financial institutions as well.

The idea behind blockchain is pretty simple. Any time that you go on the Bitcoin network, your computer is going to be hooked up to the main blockchain. You will get your own personal blockchain which is going to grow the more transactions that you do on the network. Those who don't make those many transactions will have a smaller blockchain and those who do a lot of transactions are going to see a lot larger blockchain.

So how does the blockchain work? We have learned a bit about this before, and the process is pretty simple to work with. When you do a transaction on the Bitcoin or another network, the blockchain is designed to hold onto this information. The information is kept pretty secure, usually with a special code so that the actual amount of the transaction and the information of the two parties is kept safe in the process.

This is where the miners will come in. There are rules in place for how the chain for each blockchain can be designed. There has to be a unique combination of letters and numbers that are only for that particular part of the chain. Any time that one part of the blockchain is changed, the rest will change as well and this is one way that you can tell if a transaction is secure or if someone has messed with it. Miners will go through and create the codes for these chains and when they are successful, they are paid by the Bitcoin system. It is really hard to do this, but it is how the Bitcoin system, and other cryptocurrencies, will continue to work smoothly. And for a good computer programmer, this can be a good way to make money.

Each chain that is found in a blockchain will hold on to so many transactions, usually more than one. You can think about this like your bank statement that you get from the bank each month that lists out all the transactions that you had during that time. Once the chain is full, which can change depending on how many transactions you do, that particular chain is going to go into permanent storage, and the system will give you a brand-new chain to start working with.

The idea is that this can keep going on forever. You can have a really short blockchain or a really long blockchain dependent on how much you make in Bitcoin and how long you have been in this network and how many transactions you go through. There are some issues that need to be worked out in this system though because there are some limitations in it. The system is still pretty new and growing, but Bitcoin and other cryptocurrencies are working to make these changes so that as the idea of cryptocurrency grows, the technology is able to handle it.

To keep things basic, the idea of the blockchain is to keep track of the different transactions that you do inside of the Bitcoin and cryptocurrency network. This can include the things you sell, the things you purchase, the monetary deeds, and so much more. In cryptocurrency, it is often about the purchases and sales, but since blockchain is able to handle any kind of financial transactions, there is a lot of potential for this kind of technology.

CHAPTER 4

BITCOIN AND CRYPTOCURRENCY APPLICATIONS

While there are technically hundreds of ways that the blockchain technology could be used in our modern world to make the financial industry more efficient and more cost effective, for the most part, blockchain has been kept to the Bitcoin and cryptocurrency world. This is where the idea of blockchain first originated because it allowed these cryptocurrencies to have a way to keep track of all the transactions that go on with this network. It has been very effective at helping to keep track of all the transactions that go on with cryptocurrencies, although there will need to be some changes in the future to ensure that these cryptocurrencies are able to keep growing with consumer demand.

Bitcoin is one of the first of its kind, coming about in 2009, but gaining a lot of popularity over the past few years as more people hear about this cryptocurrency and start to join in. The idea behind Bitcoin has been discussed already and it is shared with many of the other cryptocurrencies that you will find, but Bitcoin is one of the first and still the biggest one out there.

With Bitcoin, you are able to buy and sell products and services (although more applications such as lending out money and more are becoming available) all with a currency that is found online. While this may seem like the same thing that you can do with regular online shopping, the idea behind Bitcoin and other cryptocurrencies is that the money is not held or controlled by a centralized force. This means that instead of a government or a bank backing the money like what is found with traditional money, a code will control the money.

There isn't going to be an outside force that comes in and decides how much the money is worth or make other changes. No government or bank can come in and change the price or make more of the money whenever they choose. This is very appealing to many people who use Bitcoin and other cryptocurrencies because they like the idea of having a secure form of money.

Now, Bitcoin was designed in order to only have so many of the coins released in the beginning. So how do people get more coins? You can choose to sell products or services online and make Bitcoin in that manner. It is also possible to take your current currency, whether it is the USD or another form of currency, and exchange it for Bitcoin.

The way to make a lot of Bitcoin pretty fast and to release some more Bitcoin into the network (remember that only a fraction of the Bitcoin was released in the beginning) is to work on mining and this is where the blockchain is going to come into play.

Remember that the blockchain is the ledger that is going to hold all of the transactions that occur on the Bitcoin (or other cryptocurrency) network. When someone makes a purchase, this information will show up on a part of the chain and eventually will become a permanent fixture in the database. But there has to be some method in place that will make the information more secure, a way to help people remain anonymous so their information isn't taken.

Miners are able to come in and take the blockchain and make it more secure. There are certain descriptors that need to be in place to ensure that the chain is correct and will be recognized while keeping the information safe. The information is all codependent with each other. This means if you change just one character in the chain, it is going to change all the characters that come after it.

Miners are so important to helping the blockchain work. They are responsible for making the codes that keep this information safe and secure, but it is hard to do. This is why they are often rewarded with a lot of money, or Bitcoin, in the process if they are successful. This provides good computer programmers with an incentive to do the work to keep the whole system running.

Many types of cryptocurrency are going to use the idea of the blockchain to keep information safe. They need to have some way to show that the transaction did occur so that people are able to go back through and see this information, but they also want to make sure that no one can go through that information and see who made what purchase and so on.

While there may be a lot of great applications that come with blockchain and so many companies can benefit from this technology, Bitcoin and other cryptocurrencies were some of the first to develop and use this kind of technology. Blockchain has made it so easy for people to complete transactions, almost instantly, while helping them to keep the security and safety that they really want with online shopping.

CHAPTER 5

HOW BLOCKCHAIN IS CHANGING MONEY

When you look at the way that money has changed in the last few decades, nothing has made as big of a change as blockchain and the different cryptocurrencies that go with it. While the financial systems around the globe move trillions of dollars each day and have billions of people working together, it does have a lot of problems that can add friction, costs, and fees. Add to this that there are many economic crimes each year and it is no wonder that the costs of the current financial system are causing a lot of people go against it.

Many people wonder why their financial system is so inefficient. The first reason that it is so inefficient is that it is an antiquated system, one that has been changed a little bit to work in the digital world but it really hasn't changed enough to handle this. Second, since our financial system has been centralized, it is really resistant to any change that would make it worse and there are a lot of attacks and failures that can happen inside of the system. The third issue is that it is designed to exclude people; there are billions who aren't able to access some of the basic tools in finances.

The good news is that there is a basic solution that can be used to help deal with some of the inefficiencies and problems that come with our current financial system and that is the blockchain. The blockchain is a type of technology that was designed in the beginning to help keep cryptocurrency get started, especially in Bitcoin. It is basically an online ledger that is able to record anything of value. This would include all assets including contracts, deeds, titles, bonds, equities, and money. The idea of blockchain is going to rely on a clever code, collaboration, cryptography, and network consensus, rather than the government and banks in order to establish trust in the system.

The blockchain is so great because for the first time ever, two or more parties can forge together agreements, build value, and make transactions without having to worry about an intermediary getting in the way. They won't need to have the government or banks around to establish trust or figure out identities because the blockchain will do all of the work for them.

The idea of being able to do transactions on your own, without having to worry about paying a middleman or worrying about people knowing who you are or getting you in trouble, you can use the blockchain to take care of the transaction. This makes things secure, even though you aren't using a bank or anything, so you know your payments will go through and that anyone who is paying you will actually make the payment.

For those who are uncertain about whether blockchain and cryptocurrencies are going to make it in the future, it is important to understand that many firms that are in the financial industry, such as insurers and banks, have started to invest in blockchain solutions. Even companies that are part of the traditional financial economy see the value in blockchain and that it is going to continue to change the face of money in the near future. So why are all of these companies going towards blockchain, even though they rely on banks and other centralized options to run themselves? Many cite that using blockchain solutions gives them the opportunity to reduce the costs and frictions that go on in their business. For example, one European bank called Santander sees that with blockchain solutions, they could save $20 billion each year.

The blockchain is sure to change the way that money is used over the years. It has already provided people with an easy way to keep track of their online transactions without having to worry about going through the middleman like a bank or a government agency. Even in our traditional financial system, it is possible to use blockchain solutions in order to help expedite some of their own issues and to save a lot of money. We can only assume that things are going to continue to change with the help of blockchain as more people understand how this technology works and can benefit them.

CHAPTER 6

BLOCKCHAIN AND E-COMMERCE

For those who have not heard all that much about blockchain and other cryptocurrencies, you may be a little confused about why these are growing so much and why they are so important to the future of our economy. It has completely changed the way that e-commerce has been done and many other companies would do well to follow suit.

Online shopping has been around for some time and it is one of the preferred methods of shopping for many people. This allows them to find items that may be hard to get in their area or to make purchases when they don't have time to run around to many different stores while having it all delivered right to their front door. But while online shopping can be helpful, it is not always the most effective method.

First, there is the problem with getting money to go between the two parties. While most transactions are going to be smooth and your transaction will get to the seller and you will receive your product, there are times when this doesn't happen. In some cases, the transactions don't go through well, or they take a long time, and that could cause issues with the seller getting paid and the buyer getting their items.

In addition, there is always the issue with hackers and identity thieves being able to get ahold of the information. Some companies do have some security measures in place to help them protect user information, but it is not fool proof. Often this information is still written out including who made the purchase, who made the sale, and even information about the payment information. This makes it easy for others to get ahold of that information and make all the purchases that they want. This is one of the biggest issues with most e-commerce sites and many people are tired of having to fight to keep their information safe from others.

Bitcoin and the blockchain technology that they use to be successful have provided a solution to this issue. When you look at a chain on the blockchain, you will notice that there is no personal or financial information located in it. Instead, a code is used that will contain this information, but deciphering it can be almost impossible. This helps to make the transactions much safer and secure than before and it is easier for people to go through and make purchases through these methods.

The blockchain is also much faster than the methods used on most e-commerce sites. This is good news because it allows you the opportunity to finish a transaction in just a few seconds rather than in minutes or longer. Your product can be sent to you right away, especially if it is an online item, so you won't have to wait around and the seller will be happy because they get their payment right away.

The blockchain is the thing that we can thank for all these great changes. It has built up the trust that we need to feel better with shopping online, but where is it going to go in the future? Imagine that you are trying to pick out some meat from an online grocery store so that you can pick it up when it gets to the store. With the help of blockchain, you are able to see exactly where the beef has been during the process, including all the dates that go with it. This is pretty simple as long as each step of the way the blockchain was used for the transactions, such as when the butcher is paid, when the truck driver is paid to bring it to the store, and when the store pays for the meat. You can use it to estimate what time the meat will get there and to even see how fresh it is going to be by the time it gets to you.

You can use the same idea in retail. With the help of the blockchain technology, you will not only be able to get a good idea of where a shirt you want to purchase came from, but you can see what materials were used to make the shirt. You can use the technology at each part of the supply chain, if the company allowed this, in order to see what materials were used in the construction of the shirt and so much more.

There are so many different uses of the blockchain and it is sure to be the way that things will change in the future of e-commerce. While many people do love to shop online and may be happy with the stores that they currently visit, nothing will prepare them for all of the things that the blockchain can help with and it is sure to grow more and more each year.

CHAPTER 7

HOW BLOCKCHAIN COULD CHANGE THE FUTURE ECONOMY

We have spent some time already in this book talking about the blockchain and a bit about what it entails and how it works. But what many people don't understand about this technology is that it has the power to change how our economy works in the future. What if we were able to run the economy on our own, being able to make purchases and dictate prices without having a government agency or bank on the other side or having to worry about wasted money and time from big financial institutions? Blockchain has the power to make this happen.

Financial institutions are ideas that are still available in the technological world of today, but they are really considered old ideas. Some of their processes have accelerated with the help of the Internet and it is now possible for most account holders to perform their own financial transactions without needing to even talk to the people at these financial institutions. The money that is found in these financial institutions is also becoming virtual since most people rely on credit and debit cards rather than coins and banknotes.

While all of these things have happened, with money becoming more virtual and the interaction happening online, most of the financial systems have still not made the leap. They are still linked to the verification systems and transfer of securities that just is not able to keep up with what the integrated modern world is looking for.

This is why the idea of blockchains can be so refreshing and will start to change the way that the finance world behaves in the future. These are going to change the way that governments, financial institutions, and even users will deal with money in the future.

How does this affect the economy?

While there are many institutions that are working to modernize their ledgers, the idea is still the same as some of the old ways that they have done things in the past. These ledgers take a long time to put together and they are not always the most secure or the most accurate for these financial institutions. In fact, these often end up costing the financial institution millions of dollars a year.

But with the use of blockchain technology, some of this hassle can be taken care of. According to Santander, it estimates that the blockchain technology could help the United States save up to $20 billion in 2022, with other countries being able to save the same amount or more thanks to becoming more efficient and effective in the work that they do. There are many private banks who are already excited about this type of technology and who are embarking on their own initiatives to start using the blockchain technology to record their own transactions.

Blockchains are completely different from what you will find with the old system of finances. It was the result of many decades of refinement, which is really important since we live in a time when hackers are able to get into the old system, which used to be seen as secure. Luckily, the blockchain is set up to keep the pieces of code hidden in a hash, so manipulating the records is easy to see right away because the new hash values that the hacker would leave behind will not match what should be there.

So, not only is blockchain easier to use and much more efficient than some of the other methods that are out there for e-commerce and banking, it is also a lot more secure. Blockchain can add in an air of total transparency that is hard with some of the other options, but which is important in our online modern world.

Now let's say that you want to do a transaction with someone who lives in another country. With the current system, you would need to work with several other agents, such as a virtual payment platform or another bank in order to make this happen. This can be expensive and will take a long time for the transaction to finish. But in a world where blockchain is used as part of the economy, you would not need to keep the financial institutions around because the algorithms that are used with blockchain will be able to validate all transactions, even ones that happen between you and someone in another country. And if everyone has confidence in this system and how it works, the system will basically be a regulator all its own.

As you can see, there are many ways that the blockchain technology can make a big difference in the economy of the future. It can make transactions faster to complete, makes it easier to trade with people who may be in other countries, and has a lot of the security that other companies and online stores just are not able to provide at this time.

Now, the technology does need to have a little bit more work on it. Bitcoin is one of the primary users of this technology right now and they do have some issues with hackers and criminals being able to get on and use the system and the ledger to their own use. But because there is a good legacy of confidence in the system through cryptocurrency, there is also some encryption that will allow many transactions to be transparent and reliable between all of the parties. This seems to show that if the same level of trust is shown in the financial world, it could easily become the future we are looking for in our economy.

CHAPTER 8

WHAT ARE AUTONOMOUS AGENTS

Now it is time to get a little information about coding and some of the terms that help to make codes work in a certain way. For our purposes, the autonomous agent is going to refer to any entity that can make its own choices about how it should act in its current environment. It can make these decisions without having influence from a global plan or a leader.

This can be a big conceptual leap because instead of having a box that sits inside its boundaries and can't be pushed until something else, like another box, pushes it, we are going to create a box that has the desire and the ability to leap out of the way when it sees another box falling if it wants. While our way of thinking to make the autonomous agent work is way different, the base of the code is barely going to change at all.

Working with these autonomous agents can be a great way to design a code to work for you. These agents are going to be intelligent enough to work on the owner's behalf, but they won't need the owner to be there telling them what to do all of the time.

The code is set up to tell the agents how to act so the work gets done without the owners.

These agents will often be a system that is situated in, and part of, a natural or technical environment, and that system will be able to sense the environment that is around them. Once the agent notices what is going on in the environment, it will decide what actions it should take and will follow its own agenda. The agenda that the agent should follow will evolve from the programmed goals so it should act the way that the programmer designed.

These agents can be an important part of working with the blockchain. Remember that when a transaction is completed on the network, the blockchain is going to take that information and add it to the records. These autonomous agents could be designed to help finish these transactions without the owner being around telling them what to do. These, when designed properly, can help speed up the process. The agents are good at making sure that the whole system works the way that you want.

When you are looking into autonomous agents, there are three components that we should keep in mind while creating one. These include:

- These agents are going to have a limited ability in order to perceive their environment. But what does this mean for us? We are going to be able to create these agents by using programming techniques that allow for objects to store references to some other objects so that they can technically "perceive" their environment. You have to remember that the word limited is important here. While it may seem more fun to just let the agent have any power of perception that it wants, having a few limitations can be a good thing. Even in real life, objects and things will only have so much awareness. For example, an insect is only going to notice the smells and the sights that are near it, not everything in the whole world.

- If you are working on one of these agents and you aren't sure about the types of limitations that you should give to your agent, you do have the possibility of messing around and trying things out. If something doesn't work out well, you can set that limitation into the mix to get the autonomous agent to work the way that you want it to.

- The second thing that we need to remember about autonomous agents is that they are able to process the information that comes in their environment and then calculate an action. This is going to be the easy part to work on in the code because the action is going to be a force. The environment might be able to tell your agent that there is something coming at them, such as a scary shark, and then the action of that agent is going to be to move in the other direction. The action that your agent does will often depend on the type of code that you are using and what program is written, but it will make sense based on what the agent should be doing.

- The third thing that you should remember about these autonomous agents is that they don't have a leader. This principle is not going to be as important as some of the others. Many examples of working with autonomous agents will show that they have no leader because they can often work with a group like behavior.

CHAPTER 9

DISTRIBUTED AUTONOMOUS AGENTS AND ITS DANGERS

Distributed autonomous agents is another subfield of the blockchain that we can work with. It is considered a subfield of research in artificial intelligence and the point of this field is the development of many distributed solutions for some complex problems that need intelligence. It is often related to its predecessor of multi-agent systems, which is what we discussed in the previous chapter.

The distributed agent is going to be an approach to working on complex decision making, planning, and learning problems. It is considered parallel and this means that it is able to exploit some large-scale computations in a short amount of time. This basically makes it simple for the program to take care of large sets of data that humans may not be able to get through very efficiently, such as what needs to happen with blockchain.

The system is going to work with the autonomous learning agents that will be distributed on a really large scale. These nodes have the ability to work independently and there are some partial solutions that will be integrated with some communication that happens between the nodes, often at different times.

The nice thing about these systems is that they don't need to have all the data in order to be added into one location, compared to some of the other systems that have to really know all the information to be successful. This means that the distributed agents will often operate without needing to understand everything that is going on and they can operate with hashed impressions or even sub-samples and you can update them while they are being executed.

The Goals

The main goal of working with these systems is to allow them to work on perception, learning, planning, and reasoning problems. They are especially useful

if you are working with large amounts of data because you can give the problem out to a few agents to speed up the process. For this system to work, though, there need to be a few things in place including:

- A distributed system that has computations that are elastic and robust. This computation needs to be on failing and unreliable resources that can be coupled together loosely.
- The actions and the communication of the nodes need to be coordinated.
- Subsamples of bigger sets of data and the help of online machine learning.

The goals of this type of autonomous agent can really help you to get a lot of problems done in your program or on your code. There are actually quite a few reasons why you would want to use the distributed agents including:

Multi-agent based simulation: this is a branch of distributed autonomous agents that will build foundations for any simulations that need to analyze your phenomena on two levels, such as at the micro and the macro level. This is important in many social simulation scenarios.

- Distributed problem solving: the concept of these autonomous agents that are able to communicate with each other was first designed in order to help out as abstractions to the DPS system.

- Parallel problem solving: this is going to talk about how artificial intelligence, with the help of these agents, will be able to work with other computers in order to speed up the calculation.

Challenges

There are some challenges that come with using these kinds of agent. Some of them include:

- How to carry out the interaction and communication of the agents so that they work out well together. You also have to decide what protocols and language you want to use for this communication to occur.

- How to ensure that the coherency of these agents stays together.

- How to get the results from these agents to print out and make sense.

When working with blockchain, these agents can really make a difference in how the work is going to get done. No one is able to go through and manually take care of all the work that the blockchain is supposed to do, especially as the technology grows and more people start to use it. These distributed agents are able to take the information that they are given and handle all the transactions that go through.

But there are times when these agents are not going to work the way that is expected. What happens if the communication between the agents doesn't work or there is something that gets in the way? These transactions can be slowed down and may not even get through. The blockchain is meant to be fast and efficient so that users can see them appear almost right away. But if the agents don't work the way that they should, this can slow down the system and will take some of the trust out of the system.

Another issue is, what is going to happen if a hacker or someone else is able to get into these agents? While the blockchain is set up to make it difficult for someone to get ahold of the information that is inside the transactions, it is possible for them to get ahold of these autonomous agents. Messing with the code can change the way that these agents react inside the program, and this could cause some harm to the whole system of the blockchain.

These autonomous agents can be great for working on the complex system that is the blockchain technology, but it is important to make sure that they are designed properly and that they are able to communicate with each other throughout the process, or there could be some issues with how it all works out. But with the right security and the assurance that the agents are designed properly, everything will come together well.

CHAPTER 10

A POSSIBLE FUTURE "SKYNET"

This book has spent quite a bit of time talking about the different technologies that come with the blockchain and how it is making a change in our economy and the way that we will conduct business in the future. Many people wonder if this kind of technology could start to take on a more science fiction theme to it, bringing to life things that were once reserved for the movies. In the past few chapters, we spent time talking about autonomous agents, which are basically agents that are able to look at their environment and decide what they should do without the help of the owner or the programmer. What else will technology be able to do in the future?

One possibility that some are considering is the future Skynet. Skynet, right now, is a fictional artificial general intelligence that is conscious and able to make its own decisions. This is a system that is one of the features in the Terminator movies and is actually the main antagonist for how it reacts throughout the movie series. The Skynet is able to use artificial intelligence in order to make decisions, just like a human, but it is often going to have some limitations based on the program it was originally given. And since it is artificial intelligence, it is not going to have some of the constraints that come with humans, such as confusion, emotions, and attachments.

While Skynet was originally saved for science fiction movies, there are actually places in our world that already use this kind of technology. In fact, it is more real than most people realize at this time, and with the advent of blockchain and the rise of other technology, it is a real possibility in our future. Let's take a look at some of the ways that Skynet is already more real than we realize.

The military uses it

Artificial intelligence, which is the backbone to the whole idea of Skynet, is capable of doing a lot of good and a lot of harm all at once. This is why it has been very controversial when used in military applications. Drones and battlefield robots are science fiction type products that are already in use with the military, as is technology like HAL, which is a suit that will give one man the power of ten. Some people believe that these developments are a sign that an arms race is happening among nations to see who is able to develop artificial intelligence the fastest and use it the most effectively.

This kind of technology has begun to be a central figure in international conversations about how modern war should be conducted. Many of these robots and drones are set up to make an autonomous kill decision without any kind of human intervention, which can make them effective on the battlefield, but how do you get them to stop or not kill the wrong side?

One type of weapon that NSA has designed and is becoming really controversial is the MonsterMind. This is a type of system that is able to intercept all of the United States' digital communications while also identifying threats and then launching strikes without someone being there to check the messages or find out whether or not there is really a threat present. But how does the program determine this and what happens if it is wrong or goes out of control from the program? If this doesn't sound like the Skynet we have come to know from the Terminator movies, then what is?

It is changing quickly

According to the famous Moore's Law, it is estimated that computing power is able to double about every eighteen months. If this holds true and things keep steady, it is possible that a computer would end up having the same type of computing power as the human brain as early as 2025.

There are many scientists who believe that the ideas behind Moore's Law will break down before it gets to this point so we have nothing to worry about, there are already computers available that are lightning fast in their processing power. How fast are their computers? It is already estimated that the fastest supercomputer in the world is at 34^16 cps while the human brain is able to do 10^16.

It is getting smarter

Artificial intelligence is getting faster and faster at the things that it can do. But one challenge with this intelligence is that it is working on how to develop complex processing in a way that is as easy as the human brain. Right now, the human brain can take on some of these complex processing tasks pretty easily, but the artificial intelligence has some trouble doing this.

For a computer, multiplying together two 10-digit numbers right away is really easy. On the other hand, looking at a dog and figuring out whether that animal is a canine or a feline is going to be hard for it to handle. This is where the Turing Test was developed in order to measure how well a machine is able to exhibit behavior that is intelligent and similar to that of a human.

Among the various tech companies who are trying to pass the Turing Test, Google is one of the leaders in AI. So far Google has invested hundreds of millions of dollars into the DeepMind company and other robotics companies to help spur this all along. Some of the inventions that are under the Google name include ladder climbing robots, robotic pets, and cars that can self-drive.

It looks like us

There are now even some robots from Japan that are starting to look more human each year. Geminoid F, which was created by Hiroshi Ishiguro, can smile, sing, and talk and even has 65 facial expressions. The goal of this project was to make a robot that could go out in public and convince humans that it was real, and so far, it has been really successful in doing this. It may not be the same thing that we will see the Terminator movies, but it definitely is a step in the same direction.

While not all forms of artificial intelligence are going to focus on making robots that look like humans, it is interesting to know where this kind of technology is going. If it is already possible to make a robot that can do all the human functions, such as facial expressions and laughing, how much longer would it take to create some that could reason, talk, and pretty much be human other than they are run by a computer? It is pretty interesting to think about and the technology that is behind all of this science is shaping our future already.

Elite opposition is forming to it

There is quite a bit of opposition that is forming against artificial intelligence and the products that are coming from this. Stephen Hawking is one opponent of artificial intelligence and has been quoted as saying "The development of full artificial intelligence could spell the end of the human race."

Hawkings is not the only scientist and tech innovator that is worked about the safety of using artificial intelligence. They believe that as this technology starts to progress more towards having the same intelligence as humans, it could pose a big threat to humans.

For the most part, this type of artificial intelligence is not used so far to harm other people and it does have some limitations on what it is allowed to do. Even military drones and products are controllable. But how long is this going to last? As the technology keeps going on, is it possible that the machines and robots will start to think even more for themselves, going off the code that was written for them and doing what they would like, regardless of what is set up for them? This is one of the big worries of many specialists who are watching artificial intelligence grow. They worry that a future Skynet, like what is found in the Terminator movies, may not be science fiction anymore, but actually something that we would see in our own future soon.

Artificial intelligence is often used in blockchain and other technologies because it helps to make it more intuitive. There are many processes that need the ability to react to what is going on without having the programmer there the whole time. But as this technology gets better and learns how to process things like humans do, it is possible that a future Skynet could be the situation that we deal with in the future.

CHAPTER 11

GOVERNMENT'S RESPONSE TO BLOCKCHAIN AND CRYPTOCURRENCY

One of the reasons that Bitcoin is so popular is because it is its own entity. There isn't an issue about having to worry about what government or bank is behind the currency. This currency is all based online with a code, which allows it to be free from government interference. Many people liked the idea of being able to make money from this network or to make purchases and no one else had to know.

Of course, this did raise some issues. In the United States, some individuals were able to make money on Bitcoin and other cryptocurrencies, but since it was all done online, no one was submitting information for tax purposes, and all transactions were anonymous, it was easy for one of the users not to report the income they earned. This was a big red flag in the United States and other locations as this allowed for tax evasion, money laundering, and more without anyone being able to figure it out.

It is possible to use Bitcoin and other cryptocurrencies in any part of the world and you can do it all on the secure network that will protect your information and even your name. Many governments around the world have responded in different ways to cryptocurrency and many laws have begun to show up in this form of currency. Let's take a look at some of the ways that governments are handling the new online currency and what toll it may take on these currencies growing in the future.

The United States

First, we will take a look at how the United States is handling the emergence of cryptocurrency. A foreign sanctions bill has recently been signed in 2017 that mandates that certain foreign governments, like North Korea, Russia, and Iran, need to start monitoring the cryptocurrency circulations in their countries in order to measure illicit finance trends This bill requires that those particular governments need to develop a strategy that will help to combat the financing of terrorism through cryptocurrency, which is believed to occur in many cases.

This legislation is one step towards showing how the United States wants to start monitoring cryptocurrencies. While a crackdown may not be imminent at this time, this sanction is asking other countries, particularly those that seem to have the most issues with terrorism at this time, to crack down on the online currency in order to protect everyone.

Closer to home, the IRS is starting a war against Coinbase, which is one of the most popular Bitcoin exchange sites in America. The IRS states that Coinbase has failed to comply with national tax laws. Because of price inflation, privacy concerns, and what is considered the war on cash, many people are attracted to the idea of Bitcoin and other cryptocurrencies. But those who control the centralized banking system really hate these alternatives to traditional money in the United States and they are ready to push down hard against them.

While the IRS claims that Coinbase has been going against tax laws by helping people evade their taxes, many people think that other things are at play. If something were to happen to Coinbase in the United States, the main exchange site in this country would be gone and Bitcoin commerce would become near impossible for most people.

In the United States, the IRS is in charge of collecting information on how much people earn each year to help pay for the government, roads, and other things that people need. But over the years, the IRS has grown quite a bit and many believe that it is run more by politics than by an actual want to do its job. Many high-profile people have been "randomly" audited for speaking out against a president or other high-ranking official in government and the IRS seems to be in the pockets of big banks and corporations. Since these big banks don't like the idea that commerce is heading online rather than through them, instead of making some changes to meet this new technology, it is a common thought that they are going after the exchange and trying to shut it down.

Either way, the IRS is going after the anonymity that is found with Bitcoin. This anonymity was designed to help many people to make transactions, either doing purchases or sales. They could finish their transactions and the blockchain will keep all this information confidential. There are some people who will use this to their advantage, keeping information away from the IRS during tax time, participating in money laundering, and more because it is hard to trace their transactions when they are done on the Bitcoin network. The question remains, though, if the IRS is really going after Coinbase because of these tax issues or because the government and big banks don't like the idea of currency going online instead of through them.

China

China is taking a slightly different path to accepting cryptocurrency. Many advocates of this currency have guessed that at some time, a national bank would jump on board and start developing a cryptocurrency that they could use and the People's Bank of China may be one of the first to do this. There have even been some tests that have tried out transactions of this new online currency and the commercial banks in China.

As of June 2017, the Chinese government has still not released a statement about working on this cryptocurrency so there really isn't a timetable to talk about this development. However, other countries are also considering this type of online currency including Russia and the State of Palestine. Palestine is really interested in doing this because it would address two issues that they are having; the fact that they are dealing with a shortage in printing facilities for money in their country and the online currency would reduce their need for importing physical currency through Israel to themselves.

There are many reasons why China may be interested in developing this kind of digital currency. To start, many citizens in the country lack access to banking services throughout the country. Cross border payments are currently charged at high rates and using a digital currency will help to take away some of these fees. And in terms of helping the government, developing a national cryptocurrency could help to strengthen the Communist Party in China. The currency that China is creating would be traceable so that corruption could be limited.

The Chinese government recognizes how much cryptocurrency would be able to change their infrastructure, and instead of trying to turn it down, they have decided to embrace it and work on making it their own. They may be the leaders in this idea right now, but it is certain that they will not be the last to take on this endeavor.

Switzerland

In Switzerland, one of the biggest private banks, called Falcon, allows some of their clients to trade and store Bitcoin right through their trade holdings. This shows a big shift in how companies are paying attention to Bitcoin and how some governments may be opening up regulations in order to allow more availability of the Bitcoin.

Falcon is the first bank that offers Bitcoin right to their clients and they are remembered through history for doing so. This decision is a follow-up that has helped out their clients, allowing the clients to store and even trade the Bitcoin right from the bank rather than using their online wallets. While this sometimes has the negative of having more fees to deal with, it is often easier to use as many people don't understand how these wallets work to start with. It is estimated that many private banks and even governments will start to follow these decisions as the popularity of Bitcoin rises.

As you can see, governments across the world have reacted in different manners to the rise of cryptocurrency and the blockchain technology. The United States has taken a more control approach, trying to shut down this network so that people are not able to rely on it instead of the traditional banking forum. On the other hand, China has become laxer on the cryptocurrency world, developing their own to help spur their economy and make banking easier for people in areas where this was difficult before. No matter what take a country has on cryptocurrency, it seems to be growing in popularity and the changes that could come with this technology and this online currency are going to be able to change the world.

CHAPTER 12

CRIMINAL APPLICATIONS WITH BLOCKCHAIN

One of the major drawbacks that have occurred against blockchain is the ability for criminals to conduct activities. Criminals are able to receive payments and send out illegal products without ever being found out because the whole idea of the blockchain is to keep things anonymous. This is part of why people like to use the blockchain so much, but this can make it really hard to stop any criminal activity that can go on with this technology.

The basic function of the whole blockchain technology is to keep information about people anonymous. This makes it more secure because you are able to use your Bitcoin or your credit card information on the network and you won't have to worry about hackers or identity thieves because they won't be able to read and understand the coding on the chains. This can be a welcome relief for those who are tired of regular online shopping and having to worry all the time about how people are going to be able to get ahold of their personal information and use it. Blockchain takes away some of that risk by helping you stay anonymous.

For the most part, people are going to do just fine with blockchain and will just use it to keep their personal and financial information safe and secure. But there are some people who will misuse the safety and security that come with the blockchain technology. Many of those who want to commit some sort of criminal activity will take advantage of the blockchain technology and will be able to sell and purchase items that may be illegal in their own countries.

The blockchain technology can make it easier for criminals to do this in two ways. First, it is possible that a product is considered illegal in one country but legal in the second country. Someone in the second country could easily sell it to the person in the first country and receive payment for it. Since both of these parties can remain anonymous, even if the item or product is illegal in both countries, it is difficult for anyone to figure out who they are. The transaction can finish and no one will be able to do anything about it.

There are many government agencies who try to get this information, trying to figure out who may have sold the item to someone they have just caught with the illegal product. But often the accused won't be able to tell who sold the item since everything is done anonymously and it can be hard to figure out where all of these items are coming from. And since blockchain can be used all over the world, it is hard to determine where the product came from.

While Bitcoin and other cryptocurrencies are working to help stop some of the criminal activity that is going on in their sites, the fact that some criminals are still able to use the blockchain technology to their advantage is something that is hard for them to work on completely. Unless these cryptocurrencies get rid of their safety and security features, there are always going to be ways that criminals are able to use this to their advantage.

How criminals can use the blockchain

Basically, criminals are able to get onto the network and will use the blockchain in order to do criminal activities without anyone knowing who they are and being able to trace the transaction back to them. Some criminals will choose to sell products that are illegal in their country to others, or they will choose to go with products that are legal in their own personal country, but they will sell it to others who may not have the legality on their side in their own personal residence. They will earn money by providing this product to those who are not able to get it themselves, and with the help of the blockchain, they will stay hidden.

Some people are on the other side of the spectrum and they will go on one of these cryptocurrency networks in order to gain access to something that is illegal in their own country. Sometimes they will make a purchase that is considered legal, such as a gun, and then use it in an illegal sale. They will be assured that they are safe on both sides because the blockchain will keep their information and the seller's information safe from others who are taking a look.

It doesn't just have to be products that are traded illegally on the blockchain. There are plenty of other illegal activities that can happen in this technology. Sometimes it is payment for illegal services or there can be issues with money laundering and more. While cryptocurrencies are often working to fix some of these issues, it is hard to keep up with it because if they mess with the blockchain too much, some of the safety features, such as being protected from identity theft, will go away.

CHAPTER 13

BANKS AND FINANCIAL INSTITUTIONS WITH BLOCKCHAIN

Since Bitcoin was first introduced, the technology that helps it to run successfully, or the blockchain, has become very popular. In theory, startups could use blockchain in order to provide cheaper, faster, safer, and even more transparent business models compared to what is used in the financial world by banks and other financial institutions. The opportunities are endless and because of all the benefits, many financial institutions and banks are starting to implement this as well.

While not all banks are switching over to this kind of technology, there are many that adopt this technology to help save money and to provide their customers with a better experience overall. In fact, this growth has been even more than expected and it was predicted that up to 15 percent of the banks throughout the world would start to implement blockchain technology by 2017 after surveying 200 global banks.

The banks that do implement this kind of technology, which will be medium or bigger institutions, will focus the technology on reference data, retail payments, and consumer lending. By 2020, IBM thinks that up to 66 percent of banks in the world will use blockchain in commercial production.

Of the banks that have started to use this technology, many are still working on the testing phase. They are trying to figure out how they would be able to use blockchain to help with their services and products. There are so many possibilities that come with the blockchain technology that figuring out the best way to use it for each type of bank can be difficult. Banks that choose to use this option will be able to update their data in real-time and can cut out the middleman to save money, and could speed up the time that transactions take to complete, all of which could result in higher customer satisfaction.

There are a few challenges that still exist for some financial institutions that want to adopt blockchain. It is a great technology that you can use, but not all banks and financial institutions are ready to implement this kind of technology. Some of the challenges that are around include:

- The cost to the benefit: while blockchains can speed up transactions, they are expensive to build and maintain. Before a bank adds in this technology, they need to be able to make their money back and it has to be worth their time to add in this technology because it is going to cost them a lot.

- Aligning incentives: not all parts of the financial world are going to have the same incentives. There can be some entities that will have different conflicting priorities even while sharing a blockchain. But if there aren't a lot of users, blockchains are not successful.

- Evolving standards: users want to determine the standards that are there before they invest at all. But if there are too many choices available, it is slower to adopt. Larger competitors are going to be at the forefront of driving the standard.

- Governance: blockchain would need to have some kind of governing body to figure out who is going to manage it and who will get access to the blockchain.

- Scalability: the blockchain needs to be able to scale effectively from the beginning in order to succeed. Without these, the higher energy costs of the blockchain would basically take away all the benefits.

- Regulations: regulating digital identities and the standards that change across borders can make things difficult. These would need to be figured out before building the blockchain.

- Legal risks: users who use a blockchain through a bank or a financial institution need to be identifiable entities. There would need to be some rules about knowing your customer and some for anti-money laundering to help protect the company.

- Security: since we are talking about banks and financial information, there needs to be some security in place. Banks, before implementing the blockchain, would need to do research to make sure that the blockchain they are considering is safe from attack.

- Simplicity: even though all the above need to be present inside of the blockchain, it still needs to be simple and easy for the customer to use.

These challenges are part of why many smaller banks, and even some of the bigger ones, have not decided to implement blockchain technology into their business at this time. There are many bigger banks that have chosen to use this technology and with great success. As the blockchain becomes more readily accessible and more options are introduced, it is likely that banks and other financial institutions will become more open to using this technology to help them save money and provide a better experience for their customers.

CHAPTER 14

HOW TO PROFIT WITH BLOCKCHAIN

Now that we have spent a little bit of time talking about blockchain and some of the different aspects of how blockchain will work, it is time to move onto a topic that will interest a lot of people. Many are curious as to how they would be able to use blockchain in order to make money. Remember that the technology is still pretty new, which makes it great for finding new ways to make money that may not have been explored in the past yet so use your creativity a bit and see what you can find.

There are quite a few ways that you are able to use the blockchain technology and profit from it. Some of these include:

- Build your own blockchain: there are a lot of companies, financial institutions and otherwise, who are starting to see the value of using this kind of technology in their business to save time and money and to keep things secure. If you have the computer knowledge and the time, you can create one of your own blockchains and then sell it to these companies. This one is a bit harder to pull off compared to some of the other options, but it can certainly make you a lot of money.

- Add-ons: maybe you don't have the knowledge to write out your own blockchain completely, but you have an idea that would make an existing blockchain more effective. You could build something that would be useful for another blockchain and then sell this as part of your service.

- Mining: this one is another computer programming option, but in order for the blockchain technology to work on Bitcoin and with other cryptocurrencies, they need miners. These miners are responsible for taking the transactions and writing out a code that will keep everything in place but which helps to keep it all hidden as well. If you are able to do this on your own or can use a good computer program for this, you will quickly make some good money.

- Be a salesperson: if you can't design a blockchain on your own, why not become a salesperson for someone who is able to do it? If you know someone who is building an application for blockchain or their own blockchain, you can help them to sell the technology or find a customer who would be interested.

- Investing: sometimes just investing in a company that is designing an application or their own blockchain can be helpful. You will help them to have the money to get this done and once they sell or provide their services, you will earn some of the money as well. This helps you to get in on the deal without having to have any computer knowledge in the process.

- Teach: if you are really interested in blockchains and the technology that comes with them, you can create some lessons or some webinars that can teach others about this technology. Since it is becoming so popular and many companies and financial institutions are likely to start using this for their own business and transactions, you could make some good money teaching others how to use it, too.

- Business cases: sometimes you may be more of a planner rather than one of the designers. What you would be able to do with this one is look for a problem, or else look for a business that seems to have an important or urgent problem, that could be solved with the help of blockchain technology. You can then build up a business case for them to show the business how they would benefit from adding in this technology.

- Get involved in an event. There are a lot of different events that you can choose from, like a workshop, conference, or a hackathon in the industry that you are related to. You can help to run the event or else meet a lot of other people who could give you more ideas on what you could do to make money from this.

- Work for blockchain companies: there are some companies out there who already develop blockchain technologies and sell it successfully to other businesses. You could get in with one of these companies and learn so much more about blockchains. You would get the benefit of experience that you could use later on to start your own endeavors while also making a paycheck in the process.

- Invest in the knowledge: there are always companies who are looking to work in blockchain or make the next great idea that will help them to get rich with this technology. You may not be able to design this on your own, but supporting someone else who can with your investment will make a difference. Make sure there is a good deal in place so you can get paid when they earn a profit and you can make some good money without having to be actively involved.

- Run a business on the cryptocurrency network: some people use the blockchain to help them run their own businesses. They will have their products and services available on Bitcoin or another network and then accept that kind of currency. This is kind of an indirect way to make money with blockchain, but if you are using one of these networks, it is impossible to get paid if the blockchain is not present and working in the correct way.

As you can see, you can find a lot of different ways to start making money with the help of the blockchain technology. It is often going to depend on the amount of time that you have available to use with this type of endeavor and even what talents you have. Not everyone has the talents to work on creating their own blockchain or a blockchain application, but may people could choose to invest in a company that can design these. Knowing your talents and doing some research can help you to make more money in this new field.

CHAPTER 15

HOW TO PREPARE FOR A BLOCKCHAIN ECONOMY

With the rise in Bitcoin and other cryptocurrencies for making purchases and receiving payments all around the world, it is easy to see that we are slowly moving towards an economy that is based on the blockchain technology. Because there is no need for any involvement from a third-party and the security that comes with the blockchain, it has become the perfect vehicle for our economy to get to the future.

According to William Mougayar, a venture advisor and an author, the economy of the future, the one that uses blockchain, is going to be bigger than the web economy we experienced in the past. Money is one place in our world that the web has not been able to tackle in a native way because most monetary transactions will still go through financial institutions like banks rather than from peer to peer.

There is a reason for this according to Mougayar. The banks are in business to provide financial transactions and money to people who need it. If people went onto blockchain and could do those services themselves, the banks would lose customers and become obsolete. Banks have convinced people that they are still needed, but in reality, they are simply updating each other's ledgers and getting paid to do this. The blockchain technology would be able to do the same thing, but since a third party is not needed, you could save a lot of time and money.

Right now, Bitcoin is considered one of the best-known applications of this kind of technology, but the blockchain technology could easily expand out to other areas with a bit of work. Even as it is, Bitcoin and many other cryptocurrencies are already popular methods for transferring value and there are estimated to be a good 900 cryptocurrencies readily available for customers to use.

The blockchain is all about an emerging peer to peer infrastructure that is decentralized, away from banks, governments, and other middlemen who will try to control it. Blockchain makes it easy to get your transactions done between two parties, without having to add in another party. There are so many applications of this technology and that is why it is estimated that blockchain will soon be a huge part of our future economy.

Business owners can prepare for this economy

If you are a business owner, you may be confused at how blockchain and cryptocurrencies are going to change the way that you do business in the future. You may have heard about these currencies before, but they can be confusing and knowing how you can use them to run your business can be hard. As a business owner, there are a few things that you can do to help yourself become more familiar with blockchain technology and how it all works including:

- Understand the technology and the purpose it serves: this means that you need to stay current at all times about the tech that surrounds your sector and your business. You should also take some time to educate your staff about these digital transactions and payment systems. Read the news and other things about blockchain and how it is changing and be active on online forums about the discoveries and how it will change your field. In the future, it is not just going to be banks and financial institutions that use this technology, other businesses will need to work with them, too, if they want to keep up with their customers.

- Start conversations about current and future business needs: spend some time engaging with your peers, going to conferences, if possible, and talking to your supply chain. Are there some areas where this technology is already being implemented where you can look and emulate that? If you take some time to anticipate what you will need in the future, you can stay ahead of the game rather than falling behind when things begin to shift.

- Consider some outside vendors: this new technology can be difficult to understand and bringing them into your business without help can be hard. As you learn what changes your business may need to make to stay ahead of the game in the future, consider whether you will be able to do the work or if you need to hire some outside help.

As consumers and banks start to rely more on Bitcoin and the blockchain technology, it is likely that many businesses are going to have to join in if they want to keep up. Figuring out where your business is going in this endeavor and trying to stay ahead of the game are some of the best ways that you can ensure that you are ready for this new blockchain economy.

CHAPTER 16

USING BLOCKCHAIN FOR REMAINING ANONYMOUS

When you hear about Bitcoin, one thing that you may notice is that it is a currency that is known for keeping the users anonymous. This is because it is possible for users to receive and send out Bitcoins without having to give out any personal information in the process. However, making sure that you remain anonymous with blockchain and the cryptocurrencies that use it will be a bit more complicated than that and sometimes remaining completely anonymous is impossible.

When you work with Bitcoin, you will notice that it is pseudonymous. This means that when you send and receive Bitcoins, you will do so under the pseudonym of your choice. But if someone is able to take that pseudonym and link it to your identity, anything that was ever done, all the transactions, under that pseudonym, will be linked right back to them again.

Inside the Bitcoin system, the pseudonym that you get to use is going to be an address that Bitcoin will send to you. As you work on transactions, whether you are sending or receiving Bitcoin, the address you have is going to be stored inside your own blockchain. If someone is able to get onto your system and link that address to your personal identity, it will be easy for them to link it all back to you.

Why stay anonymous?

The first question that you may have about this is why you would want to stay anonymous when using the blockchain technology or when you are working with Bitcoin and other cryptocurrencies. There are a variety of reasons why this is so important for different people, including:

- Hiding transactions: blockchain, with the help of the mining process, will help to hide the transactions that you are doing online. If you want to protect the information you use online or if you are worried about people finding out what you are purchasing online, it is time to use blockchain technology.

- Protecting personal information: personal information is so easy to spread whenever you do anything online. Whether you are using social media or making online transactions, a little bit of your personal information can be left behind, which is part of why it is so easy for someone to get ahold of your information. The blockchain helps to protect your personal information because miners will give it a unique code to hide all that information. This is a great option because you can shop or do other things online without others figuring out who you are.

- Security: many people choose to stay anonymous because they want to keep their information safe and secure. Online transactions can leave a lot of information out there for hackers and others to get ahold of and this makes online purchases unsafe. But when you use blockchain in order to stay anonymous, it is easier to keep your information hidden. You can make purchases and receive payments without having to worry about someone getting ahold of this information.

- Illegal activities: there are some people who will use Bitcoin and other cryptocurrencies in order to perform activities that are considered illegal. This could be money laundering or just selling products that are considered illegal. Being able to keep your information anonymous can make a big difference on whether you are caught or not.

- Keeping the government out of it: many times, people choose to go with Bitcoin or other cryptocurrencies that use blockchain technology is so that they can keep the government out of their business. They are tired of the big banks and the government being able to determine how much money is worth or how people can use their money and so they go online to try to keep their money safe. For those who want to keep their information safe and hidden, the blockchain technology can make this happen.

Staying anonymous on the blockchain

In some cases, hackers are able to get onto the network and figure out who made what transactions. This does take some work and if you are using the blockchain technology only on occasion for a few transactions, it is not likely that this will affect you. But for some people who spend a lot of time exchanging Bitcoin, such as those who do it as a part of their business, it can be a pain trying to keep your information hidden so that hackers and others are not able to get ahold of it and use it how they would like.

This does not mean that you can't maintain at least a little bit of anonymity when you are using Bitcoin and some of the other cryptocurrencies. It is often hard to link together an address with the personal identity of the user unless they are careless or they do quite a few transactions. The Satoshi white paper that was released when Bitcoin came out also recommends that in order to stay safe, Bitcoin users should consider using a new address each time that they do a transaction so that they can avoid their transactions linking to the same owner. This is often considered the best practice, but it can be hard to come up with a new address each time you want to do a transaction, especially if you would like to do quite a few transactions.

One way that you can choose to increase how anonymous you are on Bitcoin and other places that use blockchain is to use more than one wallet. The wallet is where you are going to store your Bitcoin and complete your transactions. When you have more than one of these wallets in play, it is easier to hide information about who you are personally.

There are a few apps that you are able to use that can help you to manage more than one wallet if you choose to do this. MultiBit is a good software wallet that works with Linux, MacOS, and Windows so you can use it no matter what computer you are using. There are some other options, but make sure that you are comfortable with the one you choose and that it makes managing more than one wallet easy.

Another option that you can use is known as a mixing service. This kind of service is going to offer to trade out your Bitcoins so you get new ones that have a different history. In order to accomplish this, the mixing service is going to take the Bitcoins that you have and then will throw them into a big pot that contains Bitcoins from other people who are using the service.

After these coins are all mixed together, you will be sent back the same number of Bitcoins that you put in, but they will be new ones that are randomly picked. This makes it hard to tell which inputs are going to connect with which outputs. Now, this is effective in theory, but in order to accomplish this and remain anonymous at the same time, you have to put your trust in an anonymous third party. This third party needs to be able to be trusted to not keep any records of these transactions and to actually give you back the right amount of Bitcoin as well. When you use a bad mixing service, they could easily run away with your coins and leave you with nothing.

Online wallets or e-wallets is another effective method that you can use to mask the original owner of a Bitcoin. There are many online wallet services that will lump all the Bitcoins that are using their service together so that when you use the Bitcoin or withdraw them, you will end up with different ones than what you started with. This is only going to work in certain situations, though. The service needs to be active and there needs to be some other active withdrawals going on at the same time. You also shouldn't take up more than ten percent of the services balance of Bitcoin's or there could be issues.

One thing to remember with these web wallets is that they are going to maintain records of the coins as they come in and out. This means that if you wish to remain anonymous, it is going to depend completely on the service provider. Make sure to pick out one that you are able to trust.

As you can see, there are a number of options that you can choose to help you maintain your anonymity when using Bitcoin and other services that rely on the blockchain technology. None of them are necessarily foolproof and you do need to be careful that you are picking out a service that you can trust to keep your information safe. But if you are careful with the services that you use and watch out for your transactions with the tips above, you will be able to remain anonymous, even on the web.

CHAPTER 17

DECENTRALIZED BLOCKCHAIN TECHNOLOGY

The energy grid that we are used to today may soon look completely different. Instead of having those big power plants sending all the energy all over in order to make it into our homes, we may be able to generate power locally with solar powers and the homeowner may become the makers and traders of power instead of just passive consumers.

If this does happen, it is going to be thanks to the blockchain technology that helps make this possible. Blockchain technology would be one of the best options to use in order to keep track of the electrons that would flow through the system. While most of us are still just familiar with using this technology to keep track and authenticate the transactions that we do on the Bitcoin network, there are so many other potentials uses that we can enjoy when the blockchain is added in. In the future, it is possible that the blockchain technology could help mediate transactions of energy through a cooperative and decentralized network.

A researcher from the Scanergy project, Mike Mihaylov, sees prosumers who will purchase and sell home generated power that would use an alternative currency, such as cryptocurrency, called NRGcoin. Whenever someone ends up with some excess power that they won't be using at the time, they can just add it back into the smart grid in your area. Then, if the consumer does need some more power, such as on a cloudy day when their grid isn't making as much, they can purchase that power from someone else in the network. Or they can sell on another exchange to earn traditional money.

There are going to be a few different advantages to using the NRGcoin. First, it is going to be an incentive for people to participate because there will already be someone in the market to take the power they produce. The second benefit is that the price is going to be fixed and added into the protocol that will run the whole system, so it won't change just because the government makes changes to the law. And third, the energy retailers won't have to spend time paying households with real money because they could use the digital currency instead to make things easier. The consumer can save that currency to purchase energy when they need it and a few can take it out if they want.

The NRGcoin will give the consumer protection against any changes in policy because the payment is going to be built into the protocol that runs it all, something that is now decentralized away from the government. One kilowatt-hour of energy is always going to equal on NRGcoin and no one is allowed to change it. Right now, one of the biggest issues against solar panels in the market is that there are a lot of regulations and these could easily change. For example, there may be a time when the government will not subsidize this power so the payback period will lengthen out and could cost them a lot. This is not something that would happen with the NRGcoin and the help of blockchain technology.

Scanergy is using some real-world data that they can gather from the Belgian energy grid to help them figure out how this kind of system would be able to work in real life. In addition, they are working on demonstrations with model villages to see how this would work using solar panels, Raspberry Pi smart meters, and spotlight projects that were able to shine some light from above. A lot of the simulations and theoretical parts are done and it is just a matter of putting this into practice and seeing how it works in real life.

Although there has been a lot of interest in using this kind of blockchain technology for energy trading, including a pilot that is starting up in Brooklyn, it is still something that needs a lot of work before it has been used in scale around the world. Right now, our energy market is highly regulated which slows down a lot of the change that we would like to see. However, a lot of the building blocks are already in place and it may not be too long before we are able to see how this technology will work in our area.

It is really neat what the blockchain technology is able to do in our world. In the past, we were just happy to get the reliable energy to come into our homes when we needed it, and now we may be able to buy and sell energy based on the needs that we have, thanks to this technology. The blockchain may have been originally designed in order to help keep track of all the transactions that occur on the Bitcoin network as well as with some of the other cryptocurrencies that are out there, but there are so many other applications of this kind of technology. A decentralized energy grid is just one place where you will be able to see the blockchain technology grow and change the world.

CONCLUSION

The next step is to start learning how you can use blockchain for your own personal uses or see how you can make changes in the way that you earn and spend money so you can be prepared for the future. While the idea of blockchain technology is pretty new, it has a lot of applications that will make it very important in the future. With our current financial system becoming ineffective and costing a lot of money, it is no wonder that a lot of companies and individuals are turning to digital money options, such as cryptocurrencies, but soon to expand to other areas, that use blockchain technology.

The blockchain is ready to make changes to the world, good changes that can help us be more efficient and get more done in the financial world.

Finally, if you found this book useful in any way, a review on Amazon is always appreciated.

Don't forget to check out our other books at:

https://PositiveImpactBooks.com

Helpful Links and Resources

Chapter 1:

- http://mitsloan.mit.edu/newsroom/articles/blockchain-explained/

Chapter 10:

- http://computer.howstuffworks.com/moores-law.htm
- http://www.huffingtonpost.com/2015/06/22/skynet-real_n_7042808.html
- https://www.theguardian.com/technology/2014/feb/22/robots-google-ray-kurzweil-terminator-singularity-artificial-intelligence
- http://www.dailymail.co.uk/sciencetech/article-2128115/Living-doll-Geminoid-F-convincing-robot-woman--facial-expressions-talks-sings.html

Chapter 11:

- https://www.infowars.com/senators-war-on-bitcoin-cash/
- https://news.bitcoin.com/us-foreign-sanctions-bill-mandates-that-governments-monitor-cryptocurrency/
- http://www.the-blockchain.com/2016/12/15/bitcoin-cryptocurrency-threat-us-government/

- https://dollarvigilante.com/blog/2016/11/21/as-cryptocurrencies-grow-more-popular-irs-attacks-bitcoin-exhange.html

- http://www.ibtimes.com/swiss-bank-becomes-first-offer-cryptocurrency-digital-wallets-still-better-2579812

- http://www.investopedia.com/news/chinese-government-developing-its-own-cryptocurrency/

Chapter 13:

- http://www.morganstanley.com/ideas/big-banks-try-to-harness-blockchain

- http://fortune.com/2016/09/28/blockchain-banks-2017/

- https://www.cnbc.com/2017/03/01/japanese-banks-plan-to-adopt-blockchain-for-payments.html

Chapter 15:

- http://www.computerweekly.com/news/450418530/Blockchain-economy-on-the-horizon

- https://www.forbes.com/sites/gartnergroup/2016/07/15/prepare-for-a-multiple-blockchain-world/2/#49f8d991878c

- https://www.entrepreneur.com/article/297567

Chapter 16:

- https://www.buybitcoinworldwide.com/anonymity/
- https://99bitcoins.com/know-more-using-bitcoin-anonymously/

Chapter 17:

- https://www.fastcompany.com/3058380/how-blockchain-technology-could-decentralize-the-energy-grid
- https://www.fastcompany.com/3058323/is-brooklyns-microgrid-on-the-blockchain-the-future-of-the-electric-system

www.ingramcontent.com/pod-product-compliance
Lightning Source LLC
Chambersburg PA
CBHW050234230526
45470CB00005B/1944